ld and truly comprehend the

become a better person with ea

us special guides to show us t

tive and how to do what's rig

lead and learn how to be stro

and His grace, was to help us

When God created teachers, h

ld and truly comprehend the

PRESENTED TO

FROM

DATE

Poems for Teachers

A SKETCHBOOK OF VERSE

WATERCOLORS BY
GAIL ROTH

IDEALS PUBLICATIONS
NASHVILLE, TENNESSEE

ISBN 0-8249-4300-7

Published by Ideals Publications, a division of Guideposts
535 Metroplex Drive, Suite 250, Nashville, Tennessee 37211
www.idealspublications.com

Caseside printed in the U.S.A.
Text printed and bound in Mexico.
Printed by RR Donnelley & Sons.
Color separations by Precision Color Graphics, Franklin, Wisconsin.

Library of Congress Cataloging-in-Publication Data
Poems for teachers / [selected by Julie K. Hogan] ; watercolors by Gail Roth.
   p. cm.
   ISBN 0-8249-4300-7 (alk. paper)
   1. Education--Poetry. 2. Teachers--Poetry. 3. Schools--Poetry. 4. American poetry.   I.
Hogan, Julie, 1949- II. Roth, Gail.
   PS595.E38 P64 2001
808.81--dc21

                            2001007107

10 9 8 7 6 5 4 3 2 1

POEMS SELECTED BY JULIE K. HOGAN
DESIGNED BY EVE DEGRIE

ACKNOWLEDGMENTS

AHLBERG, ALLAN. "Where's Everybody?" from *Heard It in the Playground*. Copyright © 1989 by Allan Ahlberg. Published by Viking. Used
by permission of The Penguin Group (UK). FARJEON, ELEANOR. "School-Bell" and "Yawning" from *Sing for Your Supper*. Copyright ©
1938 by Eleanor Farjeon, renewed 1966 by Gervase Farjeon. Used by permission of Harold Ober Associates, Incorporated. HALL,
DONALD. "That" from *The Old Life*. Copyright © 1991 by Donald Hall. Reprinted in *The New Yorker* and *Learning By Heart*, University of
Iowa Press, 1999. Used by permission of the author. HARRISON, DAVID L. "I'd Rather Not," "My Excuse," and "Last Night" from
Somebody Catch My Homework. Copyright © 1993 by David L. Harrison. Used by permission of Boyds Mills Press. HOBAN, RUSSELL.
"Homework" from *Egg Thoughts and Other Frances Songs*. Copyright © 1964 by Russell Hoban. Used by permission of Harold Ober
Associates, Incorporated. KATZ, BOBBI. "Remembering: The First Day of School." Copyright © 1974 by Bobbi Katz. Used by permission
of the author. KENNEDY, X. J. "Science Lesson." Copyright © 1993 by X. J. and Dorothy Kennedy. First appeared in *I Thought I'd Take
My Rat to School: Poems for September to June*, published by Little, Brown and Company, 1993. Used by permission of Curtis Brown, Ltd.

(continued on p. 88)

CONTENTS

SCHOOL DAYS 6

IN THE CLASSROOM 34

TO TEACHERS, WITH LOVE 58

SCHOOL
DAYS

School Begins

What a gay
September day!
Chums meeting
Shout a greeting.
School bells clang,
"Hi ya, gang!"

–Nell Goodale Price

SCHOOL BUSES

Six of them: great orange, great golden carp
Lined up at the railroad crossing, red stop fins fanning.
Each waits, each listens, and crosses in turn
Headed for the lily shoals of children.

–FRANK KOOISTRA

POEMS FOR TEACHERS

LIBRARY

No need even
To take out
A book: only
Go inside
And savour
The heady
Dry breath of
Ink and paper,
Or stand and
Listen to the
Silent twitter
Of a billion
Tiny busy
Black words.

–VALERIE WORTH

SCHOOL-BELL

Nine-o'clock Bell!
Nine-o'clock Bell!
All the small children and big ones as well,
Pulling their stockings up, snatching their hats,
Cheeking and grumbling and giving back-chats,
Laughing and quarreling, dropping their things,
These at a snail's pace and those upon wings,
Lagging behind a bit, running ahead,
Waiting at corners for lights to turn red,
Some of them scurrying,
Others not worrying,

Carelessly trudging or anxiously hurrying,
All through the streets they are coming pell-mell
  At the Nine-o'clock
    Nine-o'clock
    Nine-o'clock
      Bell!

–ELEANOR FARJEON

REMEMBERING:
THE FIRST DAY OF SCHOOL

"Write a composition,"
said the teacher,
"about something you did
during summer vacation.
Make it two pages long
and neatness counts."

I sat there
remembering the quiet
of the giant redwoods.
Even my little brother
whispered.

"Teacher,
could I write a poem
instead?"
—BOBBI KATZ

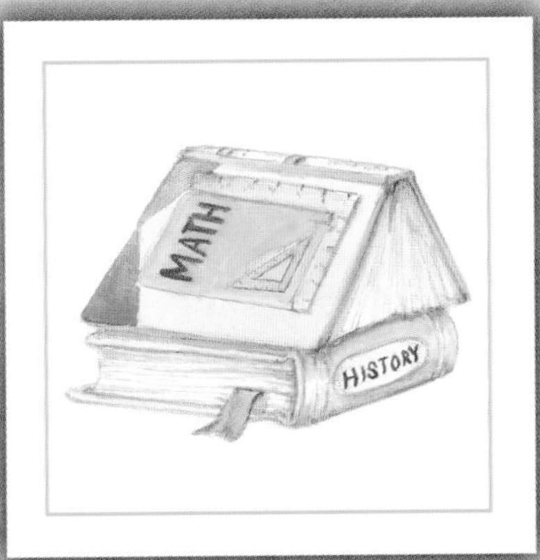
MATH
HISTORY

YAWNING

Sometimes—I'm sorry—but sometimes,
Sometimes, yes, sometimes I'm bored.
It may be because I'm an idiot;
It may be because I'm floored;

It may be because it is raining,
It may be because it is hot,

POEMS FOR TEACHERS

It may be because I have eaten
Too much, or because I have not.

But sometimes I *cannot* help yawning
(I'm sorry!) the whole morning through —
And when Teacher's turning her back on us,
It may be that she's yawning too.

—ELEANOR FARJEON

MISS NORMA JEAN PUGH, FIRST GRADE TEACHER

Full of oatmeal
And gluggy with milk
On a morning in springtime
Soft as silk
When legs feel slow
And bumblebees buzz
And your nose tickles from
Dandelion fuzz
And you long to
Break a few
Cobwebs stuck with
Diamond dew
Stretched right out
In front of you —

When all you want
 To do is *feel*
  Until it's time for
   Another meal,
 Or sit right down
In the cool
Green grass
And watch the
Caterpillars pass. . . .

Who cares if
Two and two
Are four or five
Or red or blue?
Who cares whether
Six or seven
Come before or after

Ten or eleven?
Who cares if
C-A-T
Spells cat or rat
Or tit or tat
Or ball or bat?
Well, I do
But I didn't
Used to–
Until MISS NORMA JEAN PUGH!
She's terribly old
As people go
Twenty-one-or-five-or-six
Or so
But she makes a person want to KNOW!

—MARY O'NEILL

My Excuse

But I did do my homework!
Yes ma'am!
I really really did!
Un-huh.
Mama wrapped fish bones in it.
See?
She really really did!
Un-huh.
And them old fish bones
Stinked up the kitchen
Till Daddy throwed 'em out.
Un-huh!
Now our neighbor, she's old,
And she's got an old cat,
And she got in our trash can.

See?
And she run down the street
With my homework!
No ma'am,
The old cat, not the old lady.
Now the old man on the other side,
He's got an old dog,
And he run after that cat
Yellin' awful!
No ma'am,
The old man, not the old dog.
He's too old!
Yes ma'am.
So I looked out the window
And let out a yell

And hightailed it
After the old man.
See?
"Somebody catch my homework!"
I yelled.
Yes ma'am.
Loud as I could!
So my brother run past me
And past the old man
And he grabbed them fish bones
From that old cat
And he run home grinnin'!
But we all held our noses
'Cause it smelled bad!
His hand, not my homework.
So Daddy he took

And buried it in the yard.
No ma'am,
My homework, not brother's hand.
And I couldn't do nothin' about it.
So see?
And by then it was late.
Really really late!
There wasn't nothin' I could do!
And that's purely the truth!
Believe me?
Yes ma'am!
Un-huh!
—DAVID L. HARRISON

THAT

I remember the moment because I planned,
at six in the first grade,
to remember the moment forever.
For weeks we memorized the alphabet,
reciting it in unison singsong,
copying it in block capitals
on paper with wide lines,
responding to letters on flashcards–
but we learned no words.
Then we heard: "Tomorrow we start to read."
Miss Stephanie Ford wrote on the blackboard,
in huge letters, T H A T.
"That," she said, pointing her wooden stick, "is 'that.' "
–DONALD HALL

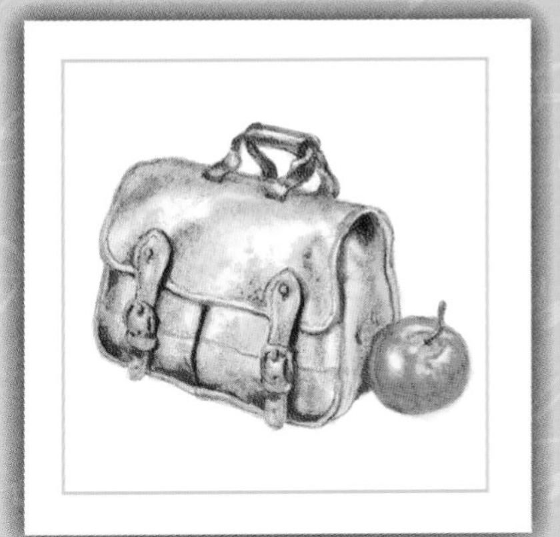

The Unwritten

Inside this pencil
crouch words that have never been written
never been spoken
never been taught
they're hiding

they're awake in there
dark in the dark
hearing us
but they won't come out
not for love not for time not for fire

even when the dark has worn away
they'll still be there
hiding in the air
multitudes in days to come may walk through them

breathe them
be none the wiser

what script can it be
that they won't unroll
in what language
would I recognize it
would I be able to follow it
  to make out the real names
    of everything

  maybe there aren't many
it could be that there's only one word
and it's all we need
it's here in this pencil
every pencil in the world
is like this
—W. S. MERWIN

WHERE'S EVERYBODY?

In the cloakroom
Wet coats
Quietly steaming.

In the office
Dinner-money
Piled in pounds.

In the head's room
Half a cup
Of cooling tea.

In the corridor
Cupboards
But no crowds.

In the hall
Abandoned
Apparatus.

In the classrooms
Unread books
And unpushed pencils.

In the infants
Lonely hamster
Wendy house to let;

Deserted Plasticine
Still waters
Silent sand.

In the meantime
In the playground . . .
A fire-drill.
–ALLAN AHLBERG

THE ERASER POEM

The eraser poem.

The eraser poem

The eraser poe

The eraser po

The eraser p

The eraser

The erase

The eras

The era

The er

The e

The

Th

T

—

–LOUIS PHILLIPS

SCHOOL DAYS

I'D RATHER NOT

To you it's only homework,
But I'm half wild with fright!
You said to write two pages
And get them done tonight!

Give me a thousand problems,
I'll work until they're right,
But Teacher, Teacher PLEASE don't make me
Write two pages tonight!

I'm really good at reading,
At spelling you've said I'm bright.
But the thought of two whole pages
Is turning my hair all white.

My Spelling Words
1. every
2. tonight
3. found
4. until
5. ground
6. right
7. still
8. fill
9. name
10. page

Test me till I'm dizzy,
I'll try with all my might,
Give me a break,
I'm nearly in tears,
I'll praise your name,
I'll shout three cheers,
I'll study hard
For a hundred years,
Scold me,
Whip me,
Pull my ears!
Only DON'T make me write
TONIGHT!

—DAVID L. HARRISON

In the
Classroom

History

And I'm thinking how to get out
Of this stuffy room
With its big blackboards.

And I'm trying not to listen
In this boring room
To the way things *were*.

And I'm thinking about later,
Running from the room
Back into the world,

And what the guys will say when
I'm up to bat and hit
A big fat home run.
—Myra Cohn Livingston

ARITHMETIC

Arithmetic is where numbers fly like pigeons
in and out of your head.
Arithmetic tells you how many you lose or win
if you know how many you had before you lost or won.
Arithmetic is seven eleven
all good children go to heaven —
or five six bundle of sticks.
Arithmetic is numbers
you squeeze from your head to your hand
to your pencil to your paper till you get the answer.
Arithmetic is where the answer is right
and everything is nice and you can
    look out of the window and see the blue sky —

or the answer is wrong and you
have to start all over and try again
and see how it comes out this time.
If you take a number and double it
and double it again and then double it a few more times,
the number gets bigger and bigger

and goes higher and higher
and only arithmetic can tell you what the number is
when you decide to quit doubling.
Arithmetic is where you have to multiply—
and you carry the multiplication table in your head
and hope you won't lose it.
If you have two animal crackers, one good and one bad,
and you eat one and a striped zebra
with streaks all over him eats the other,
how many animal crackers will you have
if somebody offers you five six seven and you say
No no no and you say Nay nay nay

and you say Nix nix nix?
If you ask your mother for one fried egg for breakfast
and she gives you two fried eggs and you eat both of them,
who is better in arithmetic,
you or your mother?
– CARL SANDBURG

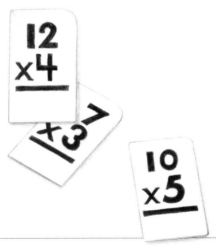

PROPPER ENGLISH

Once upon a time I used

To mispell

To sometimes split infinitives

To get words of out order

To punctuate, badly

To confused my tenses

to ignore capitals

To employ "common or garden" clichés

To exaggerate hundreds of times a day

But worst of all I used

To forget to finish what I

–ALAN F. G. LEWIS

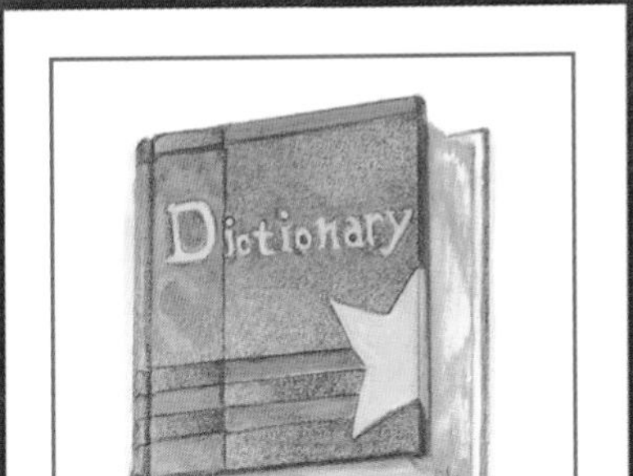
Dictionary

PHILOSOPHY

A teacher in his lectures,
Began, each day he taught,
"As I was walking in my garden . . ."
Then continued with the thought.

His students paused to wonder
That a garden must be fair
To grow such noble beauty
As the teacher gathered there.

So they went to see his garden,
And much to their surprise
It was so small and narrow
They could scarce believe their eyes.

"O sir," they cried, "how small it is!"
He smiled with his reply,
"But it reaches clear to heaven,
And how limitless the sky!

"Be not deceived by spreading space,
Mere width is never all —
The mind of man was made to climb,
For noble thoughts are tall."
— BETTY W. STOFFEL

SCIENCE LESSON

In their pond, a big old baking
    Pan, our wiggly pollywogs
At their swimming lessons, shaking
    Tails, try hard to look like frogs.

During science when the teacher's
    Back is turned, mischievous Myrt
Slips six of the slippery creatures
    Down Will Weston's undershirt.

YOW! yells Will. He hits the ceiling,
  Leapfrogs Teacher's desk, and roars
Like a lion, rock-and-rolling
  Round the classroom on all fours,

Like a jumping-jack keeps hopping
  Up and down amazing fast
Till, down through his pants-legs dropping,
  Squirmy things emerge at last.

"Kids," cries Teacher, "let's start writing
  In our observation logs—
While those pollywogs were sliding
  Down Will, they've all turned to frogs!"
–X. J. KENNEDY

Report Card

Math	A
English	B
Science	A+
Social Stud.	B
Music	A
Art	A+

Teacher's notes: A joy to have in class.

A Teacher's Smile

It seemed to me
No matter how hard I tried
It was the kid
Sitting next to me
'Twould catch teacher's eye.
My colors seemed wrong.
My lines out of place.
But yet in the end
(I think it by grace)
The teacher would stop
And stand by my desk
To give me a smile
That said I did best!

—JULIE K. LUNENSCHLOSS

HOMEWORK

Homework sits on top of Sunday, squashing Sunday flat.
Homework has the smell of Monday, homework's very fat.
Heavy books and piles of paper, answers I don't know.
Sunday evening's almost finished, now I'm going to go

Do my homework in the kitchen. Maybe just a snack,
Then I'll sit right down and start as soon as I run back
For some chocolate sandwich cookies. Then I'll really do
All that homework in a minute. First I'll see what new
Show they've got on television in the living room.
Everybody's laughing there, but misery and gloom
And a full refrigerator are where I am at.
I'll just have another sandwich. Homework's very fat.

—RUSSELL HOBAN

TEACHER, PLEASE TRUST ME

I know the answer,
Truly I do.

I know the answer,
But it's up to you
        To trust me on this.

I know the answer.
But my knees do shake.

I know the answer.
But please don't make
Me go to the board.

I know the answer,
Truly I do.

And one more answer,
The conclusion foregone:
I'll forget the answer
When the pressure's on.

Please trust me on this.
—JULIE K. LUNENSCHLOSS

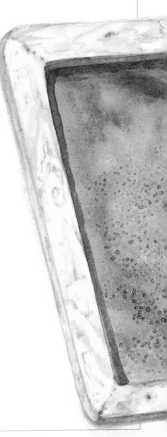

LAST NIGHT

Last night I knew the answers.
Last night I had them pat.
Last night I could have told you
Every answer, just like that!
Last night my brain was cooking.
Last night I got them right.
Last night I was a genius.
So where were you last night!

—DAVID L. HARRISON

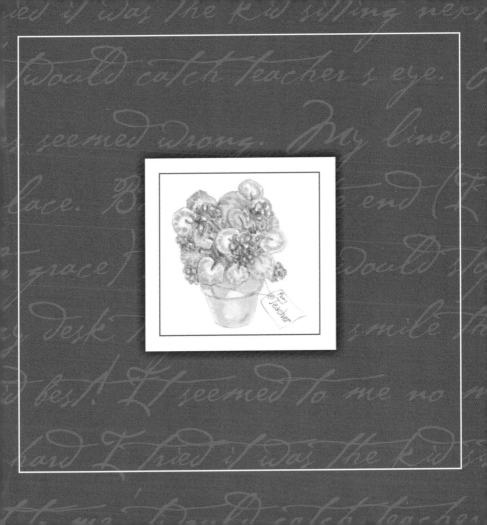

THE LETTERS AT SCHOOL

One day the letters went to school,
    And tried to learn each other;
They got so mixed 'twas really hard
    To pick out one from t' other.

A went in first, and Z went last;
    The rest all were between them,–
    K, L, and M, and N, O, P–
        I wish you could have seen them!

B, C, D, E and J, K, L,
Soon jostled well their betters;
Q, R, S, T–I grieve to say–
Were very naughty letters.

Of course, ere long, they came to words–
What else could be expected?
Till E made D, J, C and T
Decidedly dejected.

Now, through it all, the Consonants
Were rudest and uncouthest,
While all the pretty Vowel girls
Were certainly the smoothest.

And simple U kept far from Q,
  With face demure and moral,
"Because," she said, "we are, we two,
  So apt to start a quarrel!"

But spiteful P said, "Pooh for U!"
  (Which made her feel quite bitter),
And, calling O, L, E to help,
  He really tried to hit her.

Cried A, "Now E and C, come here!
  If both will aid a minute,
Good P will join in making peace,
  Or else the mischief's in it."

And smiling E, the ready sprite,
　　Said, "Yes, and count me double."
This done, sweet *peace* shone o'er the scene,
　　And gone was all the trouble!

Meanwhile, when U and P made up,
　　The Cons'nants looked about them,
And kissed the Vowels, for, you see,
　　They couldn't do without them.
—MARY MAPES DODGE

To
Teachers,
with Love

Teachers

Teachers,
who educate children,
deserve more honor than parents,
who merely gave them birth;
for the latter provided mere life,
while the former ensure a good life.

–Aristotle

WHY GOD CREATED TEACHERS

When God created teachers,
He gave us special friends
To help us understand His world
And truly comprehend
The beauty and the wonder
Of everything we see,
And become a better person
　　With each discovery.

　When God created teachers,
He gave us special guides
To show us ways in which to grow
So we can all decide

How to live and how to do
What's right instead of wrong,
To lead us so that we can lead
And learn how to be strong.

Why God created teachers,
In His wisdom and His grace,
Was to help us learn to make our world
 A better, wiser place.
—AUTHOR UNKNOWN

FOR THE TEACHERS WHO CHERISH

"Suffer the Little Children . . .
For of such is the Kingdom of Heaven."
The privilege to teach is God-given.
Like a jewel that rests in the hands —
A talent. With use it expands,
Till finally we see the dim traces
Of God in uplifted faces.

Without vision the people must perish.
Thank God for the teachers who cherish
A vision that remaineth undimmed;
For each tiny candle that's trimmed
At the altar of truth and of right
Which leadeth man into the light.

For whoso believeth shall rise;
From the muck and the mire he shall rise!
And thru the dark night he shall be
Led upward by those who can see
Till finally he reaches the goal;
A free and unbound human soul.

–HAROLD W. SMITH

My Teacher

She was no purveyor of mere facts.
With her, grades were not the thing.
She had enthusiasm—the Greek's "Fire of the soul."
And she gave of it, and giving,
Her students caught the flame.
Building men was her task.
She told us "to dream dreams,
Build ourselves a great plan of life,
Full of joy and vision."
With her nothing was dull and monotonous.
Every bit of learning was a step to nobler truth.
"Life was a mysterious adventure.
We were growing units of a perfect entity.

We were singers of a great symphony.
We were seekers for more light."
Glad and joyous was she,
And she taught us to be likewise.
"No task was drudgery, but an opportunity for growth."
"In helping others, we helped ourselves," she said.
"We were like Millet—
Painting pictures for eternity.

POEMS FOR TEACHERS

We were called to great things."
She fed us self-reliance and the dignity of life;
She taught us to think, to breathe, to feel life!
To get rid of fear and ignorance,
And dare to go out and do.
Radiant was this woman.
Like sunshine was her presence,
And her influence was like the dawn.
You speak of "money and things,"
You who find life but a grabbing process.
Learn of her as we have learned,
And you will find a new meaning
To this link in the chain we call "Life."

—ALEXANDER WILEY

BUILDERS

Some men build bridges strong,
With bolts and long steel beams,
Whereby mankind may cross
And ford the swollen streams.

Teachers build bridges strong,
To help some child to rise,
To take on hope, press on
To a brighter life and prize.

Some men lay long steel rails,
    They run for miles, I hear,

On which the engines pass,
But you shape engineers.

Some men build towers tall,
That almost reach the skies,
You start lives on their way
To love and paradise.

Some shape bridges and roads
Which bring us safety and joy,
But teachers shape the lives
Of priceless girls and boys.
–HARRIET ANN RITTER

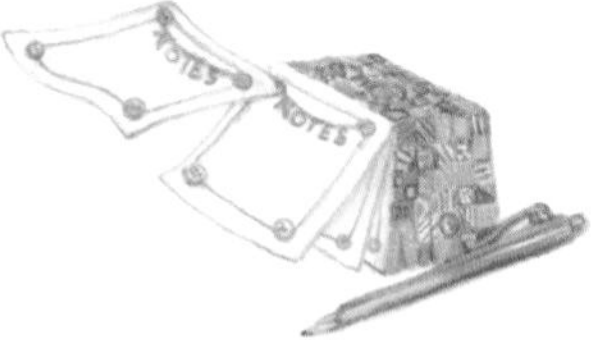
NOTES
NOTES

FAMOUS LAST WORDS

Famous last words:
How many questions?
Will there be an essay?
Fill in the very empty blanks?
Does neatness count?
Do partial answers count?
Or complete answers misspelled?
Multiple choice?
Or none of the above.

And, oh, yes.
Will you grade on the curve?
A measure of greatness
Is your infinite patience
With famous last words.
—JULIE K. LUNENSCHLOSS

THE TEACHER I WANTED TO BE

my own forever, my mother
asked home to lunch each spring,

each spring someone new:
Miss Bloss, Mrs. Kuk, Miss Michaelson never
suspecting we waited for blossom time,

hoping the rain would hold off long enough,
counting the days like notes of that year's recital piece
always I played for her, practicing

hours longer than any
hundred years' sleep any child could ever imagine:
the princess, the castle awakening, parting

branches blossoming over that aisle of tulips and lilacs, bright
promises I didn't know I was making someday
to become that same teacher each spring

on the last day of school surprised by a girl planting
instead of a secret next to the ear bent low
a kiss, so quick she never could hear what running

all the way home, crying, she all year
had listened for: yes, she was
yes, a good girl

a good
girl
a good girl.
—INGRID WENDT

TEACHERS

Paint their minds
and guide their thoughts
Share their achievements
and advise their faults

Inspire a Love
of knowledge and truth
As you light the path
Which leads our youth.

POEMS FOR TEACHERS

For our future brightens
with each lesson you teach;
Each smile you lengthen;
Each goal you help reach.

For the dawn of each poet,
each philosopher and king
Begins with a Teacher
And the wisdom they bring.

—KEVIN WILLIAM HUFF

THESE STUDENTS OF MINE

They gather round my desk at noon
In loud, disjointed fashion,
And tumble out their inmost thoughts
With very youthful passion.

They argue in convincing tones
Concerning this and that,
And soon, I have renewed my youth
By joining "verbal combat."

These students of mine are genuine,
They scorn the insincere,
And see you as you really are:
There's no pretending here.
—ALICE McPHILLIPS

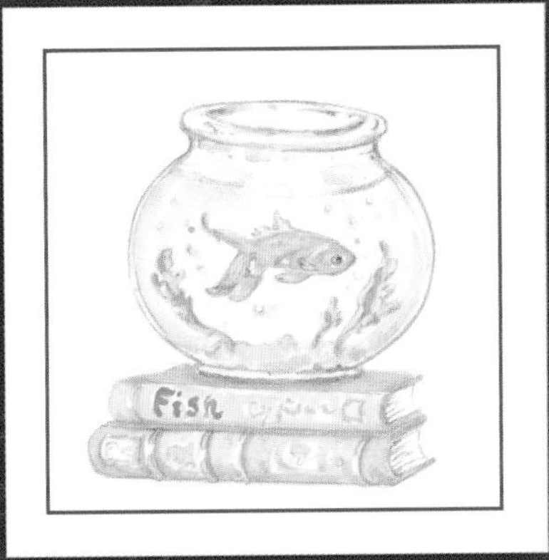
Fish

TEACHERS

You are the molders of their dreams,
The gods who build or crush
Their young beliefs of right or wrong.
You are the spark that sets aflame
The poet's hand or lights the flame
Of some great singer's song.
You are the god of the young, the very young,

POEMS FOR TEACHERS

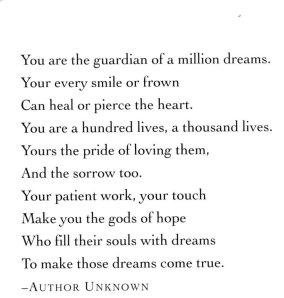

You are the guardian of a million dreams.
Your every smile or frown
Can heal or pierce the heart.
You are a hundred lives, a thousand lives.
Yours the pride of loving them,
And the sorrow too.
Your patient work, your touch
Make you the gods of hope
Who fill their souls with dreams
To make those dreams come true.

–AUTHOR UNKNOWN

WHEN YOU THOUGHT I WASN'T LOOKING

When you thought I wasn't looking, you displayed my first report, and I wanted to do another.

When you thought I wasn't looking, you fed a stray cat, and I thought it was good to be kind to animals.

When you thought I wasn't looking, you gave me a sticker, and I knew that little things were special things.

When you thought I wasn't looking, you put your arm around me, and I felt loved.

When you thought I wasn't looking, I saw tears come from your eyes, and I learned that sometimes things hurt but that it's all right to cry.

When you thought I wasn't looking, you smiled, and it made me want to look that pretty too.

When you thought I wasn't looking, you cared, and I wanted to be everything I could be.

When you thought I wasn't looking—I looked . . . and wanted to say thanks for all those things you did when you thought I wasn't looking.

—MARY RITA SCHILKE KORZAN

TO TEACHERS, WITH LOVE

Whose Child Is This?

"Whose child is this?" I asked one day,
Seeing a little one out at play.
"Mine," said the parent with a tender smile.
"Mine to keep a little while,
To bathe him and to comb his hair,
To tell him what he is to wear,
To prepare him that he may always be good
And each day do the things he should."

"Whose child is this?" I asked again,
As the door opened and someone came in.
"Mine," said the teacher with the same tender smile.
"Mine, to keep just for a little while,
To teach him how to be gentle and kind;
To train and direct his dear little mind;
To help him live by every rule
And get the best he can from school."

"Whose child is this?" I asked once more,
Just as the little one entered the door.
"Ours," said the parent and the teacher as they smiled,
And each took the hand of the little child.
"Ours to love and train together,
Ours this blessed task forever."
–AUTHOR UNKNOWN

A Teacher

A teacher teaches with love:
A love for our future,
A love for every child.
A teacher teaches with praise:
Praise that makes eager ears tingle,
Praise that inspires the weakest link.

A teacher teaches with their life experiences:
Experiences that just may reach that one sleeping ear,
Experiences that make it all worth listening for.

Teachers aren't dependent on books.
All you need are your minds and souls,
Your life and memories;
All you truly need is your passion.
–Ann Lignell Sues

TITLE INDEX

Arithmetic, 36
Builders, 68
Eraser Poem, The, 31
Famous Last Words, 71
For the Teachers Who
    Cherish, 62
History, 35
Homework, 48
I'd Rather Not, 32
Last Night, 52
Letters at School, The, 54
Library, 9
Miss Norma Jean Pugh, First
    Grade Teacher, 16
My Excuse, 20
My Teacher, 64
Philosophy, 42
Propper English, 40
Remembering: The First Day
    of School, 12

School Begins, 7
School-Bell, 10
School Buses, 8
Science Lesson, 44
Teacher, A, 84
Teacher I Wanted to Be, The, 72
Teacher, Please Trust Me, 50
Teachers (Aristotle), 59
Teachers (Author Unknown), 78
Teachers (Huff), 74
Teacher's Smile, A, 47
That, 24
These Students of Mine, 76
Unwritten, The, 26
When You Thought I Wasn't
    Looking, 80
Where's Everybody?, 28
Whose Child Is This?, 82
Why God Created Teachers, 60
Yawning, 14

Author Index

Ahlberg, Allan, 28
Aristotle, 59
Author Unknown, 60, 78, 82
Dodge, Mary Mapes, 54
Farjeon, Eleanor, 10, 14
Hall, Donald, 24
Harrison, David L., 20, 32, 52
Hoban, Russell, 48
Huff, Kevin William, 74
Katz, Bobbi, 12
Kennedy, X. J., 44
Kooistra, Frank, 8
Korzan, Mary Rita Schilke, 80
Lewis, Alan F. G., 40
Livingston, Myra Cohn, 35

Lunenschloss, Julie K., 47, 50, 71
McPhillips, Alice, 76
Merwin, W. S., 26
O'Neill, Mary, 16
Phillips, Louis, 31
Price, Nell Goodale, 7
Ritter, Harriet Ann, 68
Sandburg, Carl, 36
Smith, Harold W., 62
Stoffel, Betty W., 42
Sues, Ann Lignell, 84
Wendt, Ingrid, 72
Wiley, Alexander, 64
Worth, Valerie, 9

First Line Index

And I'm thinking how to get out, 35
Arithmetic is where numbers fly like pigeons, 36
A teacher in his lectures, 42
A teacher teaches with love, 84
But I did do my homework!, 20
Famous last words, 71
Full of oatmeal, 16
Homework sits on top of Sunday, squashing Sunday flat, 48
I know the answer, 50
Inside this pencil, 26
In the cloakroom wet coats, 28
In their pond, a big old baking, 44
I remember the moment because I planned, 24
It seemed to me, 47
Last night I knew the answers, 52
my own forever, my mother, 72
Nine-o'clock Bell!, 10
No need even, 9
Once upon a time I used, 40
One day the letters went to school, 54
Paint their minds, 74
She was no purveyor of mere facts, 64

Six of them: great orange, great golden carp, 8

Some men build bridges strong, 68

Sometimes—I'm sorry—but sometimes, 14

"Suffer the Little Children . . . , 62

Teachers, 59

The eraser poem, 31

They gather round my desk at noon, 76

To you it's only homework, 32

What a gay September day!, 7

When God created teachers, 60

When you thought I wasn't looking,
     you displayed my, 80

"Whose child is this?" I asked one day, 82

"Write a composition", 12

You are the molders of their dreams, 78

ACKNOWLEDGMENTS *(continued from p. 4)*

KOOISTRA, FRANK. "School Buses." Copyright © 1999 by Frank Kooistra. Used by permission of the author. LEWIS, ALAN F. G. "Propper English" from *A Children's Almanac of Words at Play* by Willard R. Espy. Copyright © 1982 by Willard R. Espy. Used by permission of Clarkson Potter/Publishers, a division of Random House, Inc. LIVINGSTON, MYRA COHN. "History" from *The Way Things Are and Other Poems.* Copyright © 1974 by Myra Cohn Livingston. Used by permission of Marian Reiner, Literary Agent. MERWIN, W. S. "The Unwritten." Used by permission of The Wylie Agency. O'NEILL, MARY. "Miss Norma Jean Pugh, First Grade Teacher" from *People I'd Like to Keep.* Copyright © 1964 by Mary O'Neill, renewed 1992 by Erin Baroni and Abigail Hagler. Used by permission of Marian Reiner, Literary Agent. SANDBURG, CARL. "Arithmetic" from *The Complete Poems of Carl Sandburg.* Copyright © 1950 by Carl Sandburg and renewed 1978 by Margaret Sandburg, Helga Sandburg Crile, and Janet Sandburg. Used by permission of Harcourt, Inc. STOFFEL, BETTY W. "Philosophy" from *Moments of Eternity.* Published by John Knox Press. Used by permission of E. Lee Stoffel. WORTH, VALERIE. "Library" from *Small Poems Again.* Copyright © 1986 by Valerie Worth. Reprinted by permission of Farrar, Straus and Giroux, LLC. Our sincere thanks to the following authors whom we were unable to locate: Louis Phillips for "The Eraser Poem"; Nell Goodale Price for "School Begins"; Harriet Ann Ritter for "Builders"; Harold W. Smith for "For the Teachers Who Cherish"; Ingrid Wendt for "The Teacher I Wanted To Be."